The Entrepreneur's Playbook

The Strategic Step-by-Step Workbook That Guides You Towards Living Your Dreams

By: La Rae Davis
2017

First Printing: 2017

ISBN: 978-0-692-85046-6

Global Wealth Enterprise, LLC
675 Wolf Ledges Pkwy Unit 1274
Akron, Ohio 44309
www.globalwealthenterprise.com

Ordering Information:

Quantity sales. Special discounts are available on quantity purchases by corporations, associations, and others. For details, contact the publisher at the address above.
Orders by U.S. trade bookstores and wholesalers. Please contact: Tel: (234) 421-1967; or visit www.workingwhilewaiting.com.

To Shop Other Products Visit: www.workingwhilewaiting.com

Designed by: Global Wealth Enterprise, LLC/ LaRae Davis

Printed in the United States of America

BOOKS ARE AVAILABLE AT QUATITY DISCOUNTS WHEN USED TO PROMOTE PRODUCTS OR SERVICES. FOR INFORMATION PLEASE WRITE GLOBAL WEALTH ENTERPRISE, LLC, 675 WOLF LEDGES PKWY UNIT 1274, AKRON, OHIO, 44309

Table Of Contents

SECTION ONE

My Vision Board

If you create a vision for your life, doors will open.

~ Unknown ~

3 Month Vision Plan

~ www.globalwealthenterprise.com ~

(Use this section to add words and pictures of everything you've ever dreamed of from: a million dollar check, a mansion, powerful words, your business, a healthy lifestyle, a vacation, etc.)

6 Month Vision Plan

~ www.globalwealthenterprise.com ~

(Use this section to add words and pictures of everything you've ever dreamed of from: a million dollar check, a mansion, powerful words, your business, a healthy lifestyle, a vacation, etc.)

1 Year Vision Plan

~ www.globalwealthenterprise.com ~

(Use this section to add words and pictures of everything you've ever dreamed of from: a million dollar check, a mansion, powerful words, your business, a healthy lifestyle, a vacation, etc.)

2 Year Vision Plan

~ www.globalwealthenterprise.com ~

(Use this section to add words and pictures of everything you've ever dreamed of from: a million dollar check, a mansion, powerful words, your business, a healthy lifestyle, a vacation, etc.)

5 Year Vision Plan

~ **www.globalwealthenterprise.com** ~

(Use this section to add words and pictures of everything you've ever dreamed of from: a million dollar check, a mansion, powerful words, your business, a healthy lifestyle, a vacation, etc.)

SECTION TWO

All About You

"A goal properly set is halfway reached"

~ Zig Ziglar ~

Business Goals

~ **www.globalwealthenterprise.com** ~

What is your specific goal?_____

Target date to reach your goal?_____

How will you know when you've reached your goal?_____

_____

Why is your goal meaningful to you?_____

_____

What steps are required in order to reach your goal?_____

_____

_____

_____

What barriers will prevent you from attaining your goals?_____

_____

_____

How will you deal with these barriers?_____

_____

_____

How will you track your goals? (daily, weekly)_____

_____

_____

Who will you hold you accountable for achieving your goals?_____

How do you plan to celebrate your successes to ensure you reach your goals?_____

_____

_____

What must be done daily to ensure you reach your goal? _____

_____

Strengths and Weaknesses

~ www.globalwealthenterprise.com ~

Knowing your strengths and weaknesses can help you determine whether you can complete a task or delegate a specific assignment to someone who is more qualified in that area. Instead of focusing on your weaknesses, you are freeing your time to enhance your strengths in order to get your business off the ground until your business can become self sufficient.

STRENGTHS	WEAKNESSES

PERSONAL DEVELOPMENT

~ www.globalwealthenterprise.com ~

Stay focused on your goals by keeping track of mentors, books, and things that help you grow and develop as an individual.

Top 3 Mentors (Public Speakers, Religious Leaders, CEO's, etc.)

1._____

2._____

3._____

Influential People I Follow On Social Media (Business, Faith Based, Fitness, Etc)

1._____

2._____

3._____

4._____

5._____

Books To Read

1._____

2._____

3._____

4._____

5._____

Conferences and Events To Attend (Events, Training's, Seminars, etc.)

1._____

2._____

3._____

4._____

5._____

SECTION THREE

Time Management

Either you run the day, or the day runs you!!!

~ Jim Rohn ~

Monthly Goal Sheet

~ www.globalwealthenterprise.com ~

Month_____

Faith Goals

_____
_____
_____
_____

Family Goals

_____
_____
_____
_____

Finances

_____
_____
_____
_____

Fitness

_____
_____
_____
_____

Fun

_____
_____
_____
_____

Personal

_____
_____
_____
_____

Important Dates.........

Notes

_____
_____

Monthly Goal Sheet

~ www.globalwealthenterprise.com ~

Month_____

Faith Goals

_____

_____

_____

_____

Family Goals

_____

_____

_____

_____

Finances

_____

_____

_____

_____

_____

Fitness

_____

_____

_____

_____

Fun

_____

_____

_____

_____

Personal

_____

_____

_____

_____

_____

Important Dates.........

Notes

_____

_____

Monthly Goal Sheet

~ www.globalwealthenterprise.com ~

Month_____

Faith Goals

_____

_____

_____

_____

Family Goals

_____

_____

_____

_____

Finances

_____

_____

_____

_____

_____

Fitness

_____

_____

_____

_____

Fun

_____

_____

_____

_____

Personal

_____

_____

_____

_____

Important Dates.........

Notes

_____

_____

Monthly Goal Sheet

~ www.globalwealthenterprise.com ~

Month_____

Faith Goals

_____
_____
_____
_____

Fitness

_____
_____
_____
_____

Family Goals

_____
_____
_____
_____

Fun

_____
_____
_____
_____

Finances

_____
_____
_____
_____

Personal

_____
_____
_____
_____

Important Dates.........

Notes

_____
_____

Monthly Goal Sheet

~ www.globalwealthenterprise.com ~

Month_____

Faith Goals

_____

_____

_____

_____

Fitness

_____

_____

_____

_____

Family Goals

_____

_____

_____

_____

Fun

_____

_____

_____

_____

Finances

_____

_____

_____

_____

_____

Personal

_____

_____

_____

_____

Important Dates.........

Notes

_____

_____

Monthly Goal Sheet

~ www.globalwealthenterprise.com ~

Month_____

Faith Goals

_____

_____

_____

_____

Family Goals

_____

_____

_____

_____

Finances

_____

_____

_____

_____

_____

Fitness

_____

_____

_____

_____

Fun

_____

_____

_____

_____

Personal

_____

_____

_____

_____

Important Dates.........

Notes

_____

_____

Monthly Goal Sheet

~ www.globalwealthenterprise.com ~

Month_____

Faith Goals

_____

_____

_____

_____

Family Goals

_____

_____

_____

_____

Finances

_____

_____

_____

_____

Fitness

_____

_____

_____

_____

Fun

_____

_____

_____

_____

Personal

_____

_____

_____

_____

Important Dates.........

Notes

_____

_____

Monthly Goal Sheet

~ www.globalwealthenterprise.com ~

Month_____

Faith Goals

_____
_____
_____
_____

Family Goals

_____
_____
_____
_____

Finances

_____
_____
_____
_____

Fitness

_____
_____
_____
_____

Fun

_____
_____
_____
_____

Personal

_____
_____
_____
_____

Important Dates.........

Notes

_____
_____

Monthly Goal Sheet

~ www.globalwealthenterprise.com ~

Month_____

Faith Goals

_____

_____

_____

_____

Family Goals

_____

_____

_____

_____

Finances

_____

_____

_____

_____

Fitness

_____

_____

_____

_____

Fun

_____

_____

_____

_____

Personal

_____

_____

_____

_____

Important Dates.........

Notes

_____

_____

Monthly Goal Sheet

~ www.globalwealthenterprise.com ~

Month_____

Faith Goals

_____

_____

_____

_____

Family Goals

_____

_____

_____

_____

Finances

_____

_____

_____

_____

Fitness

_____

_____

_____

_____

Fun

_____

_____

_____

_____

Personal

_____

_____

_____

_____

Important Dates.........

Notes

_____

_____

Monthly Goal Sheet

~ www.globalwealthenterprise.com ~

Month_____

Faith Goals

_____

_____

_____

_____

Fitness

_____

_____

_____

_____

Family Goals

_____

_____

_____

_____

Fun

_____

_____

_____

_____

Finances

_____

_____

_____

_____

_____

Personal

_____

_____

_____

_____

Important Dates.........

Notes

_____

_____

Monthly Goal Sheet

~ www.globalwealthenterprise.com ~

Month_____

Faith Goals

_____

_____

_____

_____

Family Goals

_____

_____

_____

_____

Finances

_____

_____

_____

_____

Fitness

_____

_____

_____

_____

Fun

_____

_____

_____

_____

Personal

_____

_____

_____

_____

Important Dates.........

Notes

_____

_____

Weekly Goal Sheet

~ www.globalwealthenterprise.com ~

Week Of_____

To Do

_____

_____

_____

_____

_____

_____

_____

Networking Events/ Conferences

_____

_____

_____

_____

_____

_____

To Call

_____

_____

_____

_____

_____

_____

To Email

_____

_____

_____

_____

_____

_____

This weeks goals.........

Notes

_____

_____

_____

Weekly Goal Sheet

~ www.globalwealthenterprise.com ~

Week Of_____

To Do

_____

_____

_____

_____

_____

_____

_____

To Call

_____

_____

_____

_____

_____

_____

_____

Networking Events/ Conferences

_____

_____

_____

_____

_____

_____

To Email

_____

_____

_____

_____

_____

_____

This weeks goals.........

Notes

_____

_____

_____

Weekly Goal Sheet

~ www.globalwealthenterprise.com ~

Week Of_____

To Do

_____

_____

_____

_____

_____

_____

_____

To Call

_____

_____

_____

_____

_____

_____

Networking Events/ Conferences

_____

_____

_____

_____

_____

_____

To Email

_____

_____

_____

_____

_____

_____

This weeks goals.........

Notes

_____

_____

_____

Weekly Goal Sheet

~ www.globalwealthenterprise.com ~

Week Of_____

To Do

_____

_____

_____

_____

_____

_____

_____

To Call

_____

_____

_____

_____

_____

_____

_____

Networking Events/ Conferences

_____

_____

_____

_____

_____

_____

To Email

_____

_____

_____

_____

_____

_____

This weeks goals.........

Notes

_____

_____

_____

Weekly Goal Sheet

~ www.globalwealthenterprise.com ~

Week Of_____

To Do

_____

_____

_____

_____

_____

_____

_____

To Call

_____

_____

_____

_____

_____

_____

_____

Networking Events/ Conferences

_____

_____

_____

_____

_____

_____

To Email

_____

_____

_____

_____

_____

_____

This weeks goals.........

Notes

_____

_____

_____

Weekly Goal Sheet

~ www.globalwealthenterprise.com ~

Week Of_____

To Do

_____

_____

_____

_____

_____

_____

_____

To Call

_____

_____

_____

_____

_____

_____

_____

Networking Events/ Conferences

_____

_____

_____

_____

_____

_____

To Email

_____

_____

_____

_____

_____

_____

This weeks goals.........

Notes

_____

_____

_____

Weekly Goal Sheet

~ www.globalwealthenterprise.com ~

Week Of_____

To Do

_____

_____

_____

_____

_____

_____

_____

To Call

_____

_____

_____

_____

_____

_____

_____

Networking Events/ Conferences

_____

_____

_____

_____

_____

_____

To Email

_____

_____

_____

_____

_____

_____

This weeks goals.........

Notes

_____

_____

_____

Weekly Goal Sheet

~ www.globalwealthenterprise.com ~

Week Of_____

To Do

_____

_____

_____

_____

_____

_____

To Call

_____

_____

_____

_____

_____

_____

Networking Events/ Conferences

_____

_____

_____

_____

_____

_____

To Email

_____

_____

_____

_____

_____

_____

This weeks goals.........

Notes

_____

_____

_____

Weekly Goal Sheet

~ www.globalwealthenterprise.com ~

Week Of_____

To Do

_____

_____

_____

_____

_____

_____

_____

To Call

_____

_____

_____

_____

_____

_____

Networking Events/ Conferences

_____

_____

_____

_____

_____

_____

To Email

_____

_____

_____

_____

_____

_____

This weeks goals.........

Notes

_____

_____

_____

Weekly Goal Sheet

~ www.globalwealthenterprise.com ~

Week Of_____

To Do

_____

_____

_____

_____

_____

_____

_____

To Call

_____

_____

_____

_____

_____

_____

_____

Networking Events/ Conferences

_____

_____

_____

_____

_____

_____

To Email

_____

_____

_____

_____

_____

_____

This weeks goals.........

Notes

_____

_____

_____

Weekly Goal Sheet

~ www.globalwealthenterprise.com ~

Week Of_____

To Do

_____

_____

_____

_____

_____

_____

_____

To Call

_____

_____

_____

_____

_____

_____

_____

Networking Events/ Conferences

_____

_____

_____

_____

_____

_____

To Email

_____

_____

_____

_____

_____

_____

This weeks goals.........

Notes

_____

_____

_____

Weekly Goal Sheet

~ www.globalwealthenterprise.com ~

Week Of_____

To Do

_____

_____

_____

_____

_____

_____

_____

To Call

_____

_____

_____

_____

_____

_____

_____

Networking Events/ Conferences

_____

_____

_____

_____

_____

_____

To Email

_____

_____

_____

_____

_____

_____

This weeks goals.........

Notes

_____

_____

_____

Daily To- Do List

~ www.globalwealthenterprise.com ~

Date_____

12:00 am _____

1:00 am _____

2:00 am _____

3:00 am _____

4:00 am _____

5:00 am _____

6:00 am _____

7:00 am _____

8:00 am _____

9:00 am _____

10:00 am _____

11:00 am _____

12:00 pm _____

1:00 pm _____

2:00 pm _____

3:00 pm _____

4:00 pm _____

5:00 pm _____

6:00 pm _____

7:00 pm _____

8:00 pm _____

9:00 pm _____

10:00 pm _____

11:00 pm _____

Daily To- Do List

~ www.globalwealthenterprise.com ~

Date_____

12:00 am _____

1:00 am _____

2:00 am _____

3:00 am _____

4:00 am _____

5:00 am _____

6:00 am _____

7:00 am _____

8:00 am _____

9:00 am _____

10:00 am _____

11:00 am _____

12:00 pm _____

1:00 pm _____

2:00 pm _____

3:00 pm _____

4:00 pm _____

5:00 pm _____

6:00 pm _____

7:00 pm _____

8:00 pm _____

9:00 pm _____

10:00 pm _____

11:00 pm _____

Daily To- Do List

~ www.globalwealthenterprise.com ~

Date_____

12:00 am _____

1:00 am _____

2:00 am _____

3:00 am _____

4:00 am _____

5:00 am _____

6:00 am _____

7:00 am _____

8:00 am _____

9:00 am _____

10:00 am _____

11:00 am _____

12:00 pm _____

1:00 pm _____

2:00 pm _____

3:00 pm _____

4:00 pm _____

5:00 pm _____

6:00 pm _____

7:00 pm _____

8:00 pm _____

9:00 pm _____

10:00 pm _____

11:00 pm _____

Daily To- Do List

~ www.globalwealthenterprise.com ~

Date_____

12:00 am _____

1:00 am _____

2:00 am _____

3:00 am _____

4:00 am _____

5:00 am _____

6:00 am _____

7:00 am _____

8:00 am _____

9:00 am _____

10:00 am _____

11:00 am _____

12:00 pm _____

1:00 pm _____

2:00 pm _____

3:00 pm _____

4:00 pm _____

5:00 pm _____

6:00 pm _____

7:00 pm _____

8:00 pm _____

9:00 pm _____

10:00 pm _____

11:00 pm _____

Daily To- Do List

~ www.globalwealthenterprise.com ~

Date_____

12:00 am _____

1:00 am _____

2:00 am _____

3:00 am _____

4:00 am _____

5:00 am _____

6:00 am _____

7:00 am _____

8:00 am _____

9:00 am _____

10:00 am _____

11:00 am _____

12:00 pm _____

1:00 pm _____

2:00 pm _____

3:00 pm _____

4:00 pm _____

5:00 pm _____

6:00 pm _____

7:00 pm _____

8:00 pm _____

9:00 pm _____

10:00 pm _____

11:00 pm _____

Daily To- Do List

~ www.globalwealthenterprise.com ~

Date_____

12:00 am _____

1:00 am _____

2:00 am _____

3:00 am _____

4:00 am _____

5:00 am _____

6:00 am _____

7:00 am _____

8:00 am _____

9:00 am _____

10:00 am _____

11:00 am _____

12:00 pm _____

1:00 pm _____

2:00 pm _____

3:00 pm _____

4:00 pm _____

5:00 pm _____

6:00 pm _____

7:00 pm _____

8:00 pm _____

9:00 pm _____

10:00 pm _____

11:00 pm _____

Daily To- Do List

~ www.globalwealthenterprise.com ~

Date_____

12:00 am _____

1:00 am _____

2:00 am _____

3:00 am _____

4:00 am _____

5:00 am _____

6:00 am _____

7:00 am _____

8:00 am _____

9:00 am _____

10:00 am _____

11:00 am _____

12:00 pm _____

1:00 pm _____

2:00 pm _____

3:00 pm _____

4:00 pm _____

5:00 pm _____

6:00 pm _____

7:00 pm _____

8:00 pm _____

9:00 pm _____

10:00 pm _____

11:00 pm _____

Daily To- Do List

~ www.globalwealthenterprise.com ~

Date_____

12:00 am _____

1:00 am _____

2:00 am _____

3:00 am _____

4:00 am _____

5:00 am _____

6:00 am _____

7:00 am _____

8:00 am _____

9:00 am _____

10:00 am _____

11:00 am _____

12:00 pm _____

1:00 pm _____

2:00 pm _____

3:00 pm _____

4:00 pm _____

5:00 pm _____

6:00 pm _____

7:00 pm _____

8:00 pm _____

9:00 pm _____

10:00 pm _____

11:00 pm _____

Daily To- Do List

Date_____

12:00 am _____

1:00 am _____

2:00 am _____

3:00 am _____

4:00 am _____

5:00 am _____

6:00 am _____

7:00 am _____

8:00 am _____

9:00 am _____

10:00 am _____

11:00 am _____

12:00 pm _____

1:00 pm _____

2:00 pm _____

3:00 pm _____

4:00 pm _____

5:00 pm _____

6:00 pm _____

7:00 pm _____

8:00 pm _____

9:00 pm _____

10:00 pm _____

11:00 pm _____

Daily To- Do List

~ www.globalwealthenterprise.com ~

Date_____

12:00 am _____

1:00 am _____

2:00 am _____

3:00 am _____

4:00 am _____

5:00 am _____

6:00 am _____

7:00 am _____

8:00 am _____

9:00 am _____

10:00 am _____

11:00 am _____

12:00 pm _____

1:00 pm _____

2:00 pm _____

3:00 pm _____

4:00 pm _____

5:00 pm _____

6:00 pm _____

7:00 pm _____

8:00 pm _____

9:00 pm _____

10:00 pm _____

11:00 pm _____

Daily To- Do List

~ www.globalwealthenterprise.com ~

Date_____

12:00 am _____

1:00 am _____

2:00 am _____

3:00 am _____

4:00 am _____

5:00 am _____

6:00 am _____

7:00 am _____

8:00 am _____

9:00 am _____

10:00 am _____

11:00 am _____

12:00 pm _____

1:00 pm _____

2:00 pm _____

3:00 pm _____

4:00 pm _____

5:00 pm _____

6:00 pm _____

7:00 pm _____

8:00 pm _____

9:00 pm _____

10:00 pm _____

11:00 pm _____

Daily To- Do List

~ www.globalwealthenterprise.com ~

Date_____

12:00 am _____

1:00 am _____

2:00 am _____

3:00 am _____

4:00 am _____

5:00 am _____

6:00 am _____

7:00 am _____

8:00 am _____

9:00 am _____

10:00 am _____

11:00 am _____

12:00 pm _____

1:00 pm _____

2:00 pm _____

3:00 pm _____

4:00 pm _____

5:00 pm _____

6:00 pm _____

7:00 pm _____

8:00 pm _____

9:00 pm _____

10:00 pm _____

11:00 pm _____

Daily To- Do List

~ www.globalwealthenterprise.com ~

Date_____

12:00 am _____

1:00 am _____

2:00 am _____

3:00 am _____

4:00 am _____

5:00 am _____

6:00 am _____

7:00 am _____

8:00 am _____

9:00 am _____

10:00 am _____

11:00 am _____

12:00 pm _____

1:00 pm _____

2:00 pm _____

3:00 pm _____

4:00 pm _____

5:00 pm _____

6:00 pm _____

7:00 pm _____

8:00 pm _____

9:00 pm _____

10:00 pm _____

11:00 pm _____

Daily To- Do List

~ www.globalwealthenterprise.com ~

Date_____

12:00 am _____

1:00 am _____

2:00 am _____

3:00 am _____

4:00 am _____

5:00 am _____

6:00 am _____

7:00 am _____

8:00 am _____

9:00 am _____

10:00 am _____

11:00 am _____

12:00 pm _____

1:00 pm _____

2:00 pm _____

3:00 pm _____

4:00 pm _____

5:00 pm _____

6:00 pm _____

7:00 pm _____

8:00 pm _____

9:00 pm _____

10:00 pm _____

11:00 pm _____

Daily To- Do List

~ www.globalwealthenterprise.com ~

Date_____

12:00 am _____

1:00 am _____

2:00 am _____

3:00 am _____

4:00 am _____

5:00 am _____

6:00 am _____

7:00 am _____

8:00 am _____

9:00 am _____

10:00 am _____

11:00 am _____

12:00 pm _____

1:00 pm _____

2:00 pm _____

3:00 pm _____

4:00 pm _____

5:00 pm _____

6:00 pm _____

7:00 pm _____

8:00 pm _____

9:00 pm _____

10:00 pm _____

11:00 pm _____

Daily To- Do List

~ www.globalwealthenterprise.com ~

Date_____

12:00 am _____

1:00 am _____

2:00 am _____

3:00 am _____

4:00 am _____

5:00 am _____

6:00 am _____

7:00 am _____

8:00 am _____

9:00 am _____

10:00 am _____

11:00 am _____

12:00 pm _____

1:00 pm _____

2:00 pm _____

3:00 pm _____

4:00 pm _____

5:00 pm _____

6:00 pm _____

7:00 pm _____

8:00 pm _____

9:00 pm _____

10:00 pm _____

11:00 pm _____

Daily To- Do List

~ www.globalwealthenterprise.com ~

Date_____

12:00 am _____

1:00 am _____

2:00 am _____

3:00 am _____

4:00 am _____

5:00 am _____

6:00 am _____

7:00 am _____

8:00 am _____

9:00 am _____

10:00 am _____

11:00 am _____

12:00 pm _____

1:00 pm _____

2:00 pm _____

3:00 pm _____

4:00 pm _____

5:00 pm _____

6:00 pm _____

7:00 pm _____

8:00 pm _____

9:00 pm _____

10:00 pm _____

11:00 pm _____

Daily To- Do List

~ www.globalwealthenterprise.com ~

Date_____

12:00 am _____

1:00 am _____

2:00 am _____

3:00 am _____

4:00 am _____

5:00 am _____

6:00 am _____

7:00 am _____

8:00 am _____

9:00 am _____

10:00 am _____

11:00 am _____

12:00 pm _____

1:00 pm _____

2:00 pm _____

3:00 pm _____

4:00 pm _____

5:00 pm _____

6:00 pm _____

7:00 pm _____

8:00 pm _____

9:00 pm _____

10:00 pm _____

11:00 pm _____

Daily To- Do List

~ www.globalwealthenterprise.com ~

Date_____

12:00 am _____

1:00 am _____

2:00 am _____

3:00 am _____

4:00 am _____

5:00 am _____

6:00 am _____

7:00 am _____

8:00 am _____

9:00 am _____

10:00 am _____

11:00 am _____

12:00 pm _____

1:00 pm _____

2:00 pm _____

3:00 pm _____

4:00 pm _____

5:00 pm _____

6:00 pm _____

7:00 pm _____

8:00 pm _____

9:00 pm _____

10:00 pm _____

11:00 pm _____

Daily To- Do List

~ www.globalwealthenterprise.com ~

Date_____

12:00 am _____

1:00 am _____

2:00 am _____

3:00 am _____

4:00 am _____

5:00 am _____

6:00 am _____

7:00 am _____

8:00 am _____

9:00 am _____

10:00 am _____

11:00 am _____

12:00 pm _____

1:00 pm _____

2:00 pm _____

3:00 pm _____

4:00 pm _____

5:00 pm _____

6:00 pm _____

7:00 pm _____

8:00 pm _____

9:00 pm _____

10:00 pm _____

11:00 pm _____

SECTION FOUR

COUNT THE COST

"By failing to prepare, you are preparing to fail."

~ Benjamin Franklin ~

Business Start-Up Checklist

~ www.globalwealthenterprise.com ~

Use this Checklist as a reference guide to know and understand a few major key components to successfully starting your business.

- ✓ **Select a Name and Legal Structure**
  (ex. Sole Proprietorship, Partnership, Limited Liability, Corporation or S-Corporation)

- ✓ **Obtain Your Federal Employer Identification Number** (FEIN)
(Otherwise known as your Tax Id Number)

- ✓ **Get a Mentor**
  (A mentor is able to guide you in the right direction or give you a renewed hope when you feel like giving up)

- ✓ **Write a Business Plan**

- ✓ **Open a Company Bank Account**

- ✓ **Obtain Licenses & Permits**
(Federal, State, Business License, Sales Tax Permit)

- ✓ **Lease Office, Warehouse, or Retail Space**
(unless you're operating a home-based business)

- ✓ **Obtain Business Insurance**
(Errors and Omissions, General Liability, and any other insurances that may be needed)

- ✓ **Develop Your Business Brand**

Logos	Websites	Company E-mail Address
Business Cards	Social Media Profiles	Trademarks/ Patents

- ✓ **Hire Employees**

- ✓ **Set-up An Account and Record Keeping System**
(Keep a system in place that can record income, expenses, receipts, etc. for tax purposes)

- ✓ **Set-up A Payroll System**

- ✓ **Assign Responsibilities To a Manager**
(Your job is to be innovative and creative, so delegate duties to a person that can report to you as needed)

Business Start-Up Expenses

~ www.globalwealthenterprise.com ~

Use this page to get an understanding of how much it will cost you to get your business started. This is a great tool to reference when you're determining how much money to ask for from investors, grants and any other outside source. This is also a great way to determine your costs if you're on a strict budget.

	Where Item Must Be Purchased From (Website or Location)	Cost	Date Purchased
Business License			
E.I.N #			
Business Cards			
Website			
Legal Services			
Accounting Services			
Professional Services			
Licenses/ Permits			
Marketing Materials			
Advertising			
Business Utilities			
Prepaid Insurances			
Salary & Wages			
Payroll Taxes			
Tools & Supplies			
Travel			
Furniture & Fixtures			
Building Improvements			
Land/ Building			
Starting Inventory			
Cash (Working Capital)			
Other (specify)			
Total Cost			

Business Capital List

~ www.globalwealthenterprise.com ~

Capital to operate your business can come from many types of sources such as: cash on hand, credit cards, lines of credit, loans, grants, investors, crowdfunding, or family and friends. Use this section to list what type of capital you have and where you will allocate your funds within your business.

Type	Amount	Date	To Be Spent On...

Business Expense Tracker

~ www.globalwealthenterprise.com ~

#	Recurring Expense	Amount	Date Due	Date Paid	Balance

Business Expense Tracker

~ www.globalwealthenterprise.com ~

#	Recurring Expense	Amount	Date Due	Date Paid	Balance

Business Expense Tracker

~ www.globalwealthenterprise.com ~

#	Recurring Expense	Amount	Date Due	Date Paid	Balance

Business Expense Tracker

~ www.globalwealthenterprise.com ~

#	Recurring Expense	Amount	Date Due	Date Paid	Balance

Business Expense Tracker

~ www.globalwealthenterprise.com ~

#	Recurring Expense	Amount	Date Due	Date Paid	Balance

Business Expense Tracker

~ www.globalwealthenterprise.com ~

#	Recurring Expense	Amount	Date Due	Date Paid	Balance

SECTION FIVE

All About My Business

*"Put your heart, mind and soul into even your smallest acts.
This is the secret of success."*

~ Swami Sivananda ~

Business Information

~ **www.globalwealthenterprise.com** ~

Business Name _____

Business Type _____ LLC _____ S-Corp _____ C-Corp _____ Non Profit _____ Sole Proprietor

Business Address _____ Suite _____

City _____ State _____ Zip _____

Business Phone (_____)- _____ -_____ Ext. _____

Business Fax (_____)- _____ -_____

Business E-mail _____

Business Website _____

Business Bank Name_____

Routing Number_____

Checking Account Number _____

Savings Account Number_____

Business Insurance Name_____

Insurance Phone Number (_____)- _____ -_____ Ext _____

Contact Person Name _____

Insurance Company Website_____

Account Number_____

Insurance Type_____ Coverage Amount_____

Licenses And Certifications

~ www.globalwealthenterprise.com ~

Licenses

License Name_____

Date Obtained_____ Date Expires_____

License Name_____

Date Obtained_____ Date Expires_____

License Name_____

Date Obtained_____ Date Expires_____

License Name_____

Date Obtained_____ Date Expires_____

License Name_____

Date Obtained_____ Date Expires_____

Certificates

Certificate Name_____ Date Obtained_____

Certificate Name_____ Date Obtained_____

Certificate Name_____ Date Obtained_____

Certificate Name_____ Date Obtained_____

Certificate Name_____ Date Obtained_____

Websites/ Login Information

~ www.globalwealthenterprise.com ~

1. Website _____

    Username_____ Password_____

2. Website _____

    Username_____ Password_____

3. Website _____

    Username_____ Password_____

4. Website _____

    Username_____ Password_____

.5. Website _____

    Username_____ Password_____

.6. Website _____

    Username_____ Password_____

.7. Website _____

    Username_____ Password_____

.8. Website _____

    Username_____ Password_____

.9. Website _____

    Username_____ Password_____

10. Website _____

    Username_____ Password_____

SECTION SIX

Your Business Plan

"A goal without a plan is just a wish"

~ Antoine de Saint-Exupery ~

Business Plan

1.0 Executive Summary
(What will you provide)

_____

_____

_____

1.1 Mission:_____

_____

1.2 Motto:_____

The Keys To Success In Our Business:

1. _____

2. _____

3. _____

4. _____

5. _____

2.0 Products and Services

2.1 Products

Our business provides the following products:

1. _____

2. _____

3. _____

2.2 Services

Our business provides the following products:

1. _____

2. _____

Business Plan

2.3 Pricing

_____

_____

_____

3.0 Market Analysis Summary

_____

_____

_____

3.1 Target Market

Our Typical Client Will Be:

Age Range: _____

Income Level: _____

Sex: _____

Employment Status: _____

Needs:_____ _____

Interests: _____

Demographics: _____

How many people in your demographics would be able to benefit from what you offer:

_____

_____

_____

3.2 Future Customers_____

_____

Business Plan

~ www.globalwealthenterprise.com ~

3.3 Market Growth_____

_____

_____

3.4 Our Competitors _____

_____

_____

3.5 Our Advantage _____

_____

_____

4.0 Strategy and Implementation

4.1 Marketing Plan_____

_____

_____

Name Six (6) Different Avenues You'll Use For Marketing

_____   _____

_____   _____

_____   _____

4.2 Sales Plan _____

_____

_____

4.3 Location and Facilities _____

_____

Business Plan

4.4 Technology _____

_____

_____

4.5 Equipment & Tools

_____   _____

_____   _____

_____   _____

_____   _____

5.0 Company and Management

5.1 Operational Summary _____

_____

_____

5.2 Organizational Summary _____

_____

_____

5.3 Supplier Summary _____

_____

_____

5.4 Employment Overview (Your Team & Their Roles) _____

_____

_____

Business Plan

~ www.globalwealthenterprise.com ~

Use this section to list each employee and their role, if you are outsourcing your available positions then list each company and their role as it pertains to your business.

Employee #1 _____

_____

_____

Employee #2 _____

_____

_____

Employee #3 _____

_____

_____

Employee #4 _____

_____

_____

Employee #5 _____

_____

_____

Employee #6 _____

_____

_____

Business Plan

5.4 Regulations (Rules set in place for employees)

Rule #1 _____

Rule #2 _____

Rule #3 _____

Rule #4 _____

Rule #5 _____

Rule #6 _____

Rule #7 _____

Rule #8 _____

Rule #9 _____

Rule #10 _____

5.5 Insurance Coverage

Fire Insurance: _____

Theft Insurance: _____

Liability Insurance: _____

Car Insurance: _____

Benefits Package: _____

Other Insurance: _____

Other Insurance: _____

Other Insurance: _____

Business Plan

~ www.globalwealthenterprise.com ~

6.0 Action Plan _____

_____

_____

_____

_____

7.0 Financial Plan

7.1 Revenue / Sales Forecast _____

_____

_____

_____

7.2 Expenses

Rent _____   Internet _____

Light _____   Insurance _____

Gas _____   Payroll _____

Phone _____   Website _____

Inventory _____   Supplies _____

Vehicle Payments _____   Vehicle Gas _____

Other _____   Other _____

Other _____   Other _____

Other _____   Other _____

Business Plan

7.3 Projected Profit and Loss _____

_____

_____

_____

_____

7.4 Projected Cash Flow _____

_____

_____

_____

_____

7.5 Projected Balance Sheet _____

_____

_____

_____

_____

8.0 Exit Strategy _____

_____

_____

_____

_____

SECTION SEVEN

Marketing In Action

"A Business is just a hobby if money isn't the goal"

~Unknown~

Weekly Social Media Advertising

~ www.globalwealthenterprise.com ~

Social Media Platform:_____ **Week of:**_____

Likes at beginning of week:_____

Likes at the end of week:_____

Total New Likes:_____

Monday

Time_____

Time_____

Time_____

Time_____

Time_____

Tuesday

Time_____

Time_____

Time_____

Time_____

Time_____

Wednesday

Time_____

Time_____

Time_____

Time_____

Time_____

Thursday

Time_____

Time_____

Time_____

Time_____

Time_____

Friday

Time_____

Time_____

Time_____

Time_____

Time_____

Saturday

Time_____

Time_____

Time_____

Time_____

Time_____

Sunday

Time_____

Time_____

Time_____

Time_____

Weekly Social Media Advertising

~ www.globalwealthenterprise.com ~

Social Media Platform:_____   Week of:_____

Likes at beginning of week:_____

Likes at the end of week:_____

Total New Likes:_____

Monday

Time_____

Time_____

Time_____

Time_____

Time_____

Tuesday

Time_____

Time_____

Time_____

Time_____

Time_____

Wednesday

Time_____

Time_____

Time_____

Time_____

Time_____

Thursday

Time_____

Time_____

Time_____

Time_____

Time_____

Friday

Time_____

Time_____

Time_____

Time_____

Time_____

Saturday

Time_____

Time_____

Time_____

Time_____

Time_____

Sunday

Time_____

Time_____

Time_____

Time_____

Weekly Social Media Advertising

~ www.globalwealthenterprise.com ~

Social Media Platform:_____   **Week of:**_____

Likes at beginning of week:_____

Likes at the end of week:_____

Total New Likes:_____

Monday

Time_____

Time_____

Time_____

Time_____

Time_____

Tuesday

Time_____

Time_____

Time_____

Time_____

Time_____

Wednesday

Time_____

Time_____

Time_____

Time_____

Time_____

Thursday

Time_____

Time_____

Time_____

Time_____

Time_____

Friday

Time_____

Time_____

Time_____

Time_____

Time_____

Saturday

Time_____

Time_____

Time_____

Time_____

Time_____

Sunday

Time_____

Time_____

Time_____

Time_____

Weekly Social Media Advertising

~ www.globalwealthenterprise.com ~

Social Media Platform:_____   Week of:_____

Likes at beginning of week:_____

Likes at the end of week:_____

Total New Likes:_____

Monday	Tuesday	Wednesday
Time_____	Time_____	Time_____
Time_____	Time_____	Time_____
Time_____	Time_____	Time_____
Time_____	Time_____	Time_____
Time_____	Time_____	Time_____

Thursday	Friday	Saturday
Time_____	Time_____	Time_____
Time_____	Time_____	Time_____
Time_____	Time_____	Time_____
Time_____	Time_____	Time_____
Time_____	Time_____	Time_____

Sunday

Time_____

Time_____

Time_____

Time_____

Weekly Social Media Advertising

~ www.globalwealthenterprise.com ~

Social Media Platform:_____   Week of:_____

Likes at beginning of week:_____

Likes at the end of week:_____

Total New Likes:_____

Monday

Time_____

Time_____

Time_____

Time_____

Time_____

Tuesday

Time_____

Time_____

Time_____

Time_____

Time_____

Wednesday

Time_____

Time_____

Time_____

Time_____

Time_____

Thursday

Time_____

Time_____

Time_____

Time_____

Time_____

Friday

Time_____

Time_____

Time_____

Time_____

Time_____

Saturday

Time_____

Time_____

Time_____

Time_____

Time_____

Sunday

Time_____

Time_____

Time_____

Time_____

Sales Projections/ Actual

~ www.globalwealthenterprise.com ~

Week of:_____

What is your sales goal for the week:_____

How many products/ services must be sold to reach that goal:_____

Date	Product/ Service Sold	Quantity	Cost	Profit

Total Products/ Services Sold:_____

Did you meet your sales goal for the week?   Yes   No

How can you make next week more profitable?_____

Sales Projections/ Actual

~ www.globalwealthenterprise.com ~

Week of:_____

What is your sales goal for the week:_____

How many products/ services must be sold to reach that goal:_____

Date	Product/ Service Sold	Quantity	Cost	Profit

Total Products/ Services Sold:_____

Did you meet your sales goal for the week?   Yes   No

How can you make next week more profitable?_____

Sales Projections/ Actual

~ www.globalwealthenterprise.com ~

Week of:_____

What is your sales goal for the week:_____

How many products/ services must be sold to reach that goal:_____

Date	Product/ Service Sold	Quantity	Cost	Profit

Total Products/ Services Sold:_____

Did you meet your sales goal for the week?   Yes   No

How can you make next week more profitable?_____

Sales Projections/ Actual

~ www.globalwealthenterprise.com ~

Week of:_____

What is your sales goal for the week:_____

How many products/ services must be sold to reach that goal:_____

Date	Product/ Service Sold	Quantity	Cost	Profit

Total Products/ Services Sold:_____

Did you meet your sales goal for the week?   Yes   No

How can you make next week more profitable?_____

Sales Projections/ Actual

~ www.globalwealthenterprise.com ~

Week of:_____

What is your sales goal for the week:_____

How many products/ services must be sold to reach that goal:_____

Date	Product/ Service Sold	Quantity	Cost	Profit

Total Products/ Services Sold:_____

Did you meet your sales goal for the week?   Yes   No

How can you make next week more profitable?_____